Dolley Madison, the White House, and the Big Tornado

by Alice Boynton and Wiley Blevins

illustrated by Massimiliano di Lauro

Wednesday, August 24, 1814
Dawn

Dolley Madison races up the White House stairs clutching her spyglass. She peers out at the road, turning in one direction and then another. Where is her husband? Is her dear James approaching? But no, President James Madison is not in sight. All she sees are carriages and carts piled high with trunks and bedding. All she hears is the pounding of horses' hooves as their frantic drivers urge them away from the city of Washington— *faster, faster!*

A glance at the red-streaked sky tells her it will be another scorching day. Little does she know the sky will not be the only thing on fire this day.

The British army is back! Not so long ago, they lost the Revolutionary War, and an independent United States was founded. Now the two countries are at war again. And this time the British are determined to win. Their warships have landed at the Chesapeake Bay, and their troops are on the move. Leading the way is Admiral George Cockburn (KOH-burn), mounted high on his white horse. He is so hated by the Americans that there is a reward of $1,000 for his head—or $500 for each ear. But Cockburn is a hero to his men. And so they march. Every day without breaks. Roasting in their red woolen uniforms.

Their destination: Washington.
Their goal: Destroy it.

Panic spreads in the capital city. Which direction are the British coming from? No one knows. But the British are coming. That they are sure of.

It is the middle of the night. The Smith family awakens to loud knocking and a voice crying out, "The enemy are advancing . . . Go, for God's sake, go." Margaret Bayard Smith, Dolley's good friend, rouses her daughters—ages 3, 10, and 13—and her servants. They load a wagon with goods and prepare the carriage and horses. Quickly, quickly. Just before dawn, they flee. Are the girls afraid? Not a bit.

What a hullabaloo. What an adventure!

As the Smith family awakens, so do Admiral Cockburn and General Robert Ross. A messenger arrives at their camp with urgent orders: DO NOT ATTACK. The troops are to return to their ships. IMMEDIATELY. Cockburn is shocked. He is so close to his prize— Washington! No, he will not obey the orders. The two leaders argue for hours, but Cockburn is determined. Finally, Ross agrees. At dawn, they will march their troops as planned.

Wednesday, August 24, 1814
Morning

It's Wednesday, a day all of Washington looks forward to. Every Wednesday, Dolley opens the White House to one and all. It's their chance to meet and greet. To talk politics. People cram into the rooms, oohing and aahing. Upon entering, they are greeted by a life-size painting of George Washington. Squeezing into the next room, they admire the red velvet drapes framing the tall windows. So elegant. They exclaim over the latest treat—ice cream. Delicious! And moving among her guests is Dolley. She chats with everyone. The tall feathers in Dolley's turban rise above the heads of the crowd. People elbow one another. *There's the presidentess!* She is easy to spot.

But on this Wednesday, Dolley wonders if there is anyone left in Washington to show up.

Rumors fly that Admiral Cockburn will make Dolley his prisoner when he attacks Washington. People whisper that he will parade her through the streets of London. Imagine, the beloved wife of the president—a war prize!

As the British march toward Washington from the south, American soldiers close in from the north. Private John Pendleton Kennedy hobbles under the broiling sun. His feet are swollen and they ache after his three-day march from Baltimore, Maryland. When his regiment stops for the night, the 18-year-old changes his boots for a pair of soft, fancy shoes. Perfect for dancing. But why bring fancy shoes to war? He thinks that "after we [have] beaten the British army and saved Washington, Mr. Madison would very likely invite us to a ball at the White House."

Kennedy is fast asleep when the drums suddenly sound the alarm. The enemy is near! In all the hustle and bustle to move out, he can't find his army boots. He has no choice but to line up wearing his dancing shoes.

Like Private Kennedy, Lieutenant George Gleig is 18 years old. But unlike Kennedy, Gleig has fought in wars before. Even so, he writes in his journal that he cannot remember a time when he "suffered more severely from heat and fatigue." But he is proud to serve under Admiral Cockburn and General Ross, and he marches on, sweating in his woolen uniform. Coughing from the clouds of dust flying in his face. And weighed down by the load he carries on his back: his weapons, ammunition, clothing, food, water. There are no horses to ride, no mules to carry supplies.

It won't be long before these two young soldiers clash in a battle for Washington. Will they both survive?

The capital is strangely quiet. All Dolley's friends are gone. Mrs. Smith and her family have fled. Dolley's husband, President James Madison, is on the battlefield meeting with his generals. Even the one hundred guards assigned to protect her and the White House have run off. But Dolley digs in her heels. She won't leave, not "until I see Mr. Madison safe." The determined presidentess stays in the White House with only the servants and Polly, her pet macaw.

The temperature climbs to 100 degrees. Still, the 5,000 dusty and thirsty British troops trudge on. Closer and closer to Washington.

With James away, it's up to Dolley to pack. Worried about her safety, he has written that she must be ready to leave the city at a moment's notice. Dolley fills trunk after trunk with important government papers and a copy of the Declaration of Independence. They must be saved. Just in case. She adds some of the White House silver and the precious red velvet drapes. But there are not enough wagons to hold personal belongings. Unfortunately, they will be left behind.

Despite the warnings, Dolley is fearless. She remains in the White House. "If I could have had a cannon through every window . . . " Dolley later writes. She would do anything to stop the British and save America's most important home.

The British have been marching through the night, but in the morning they are surprisingly cheerful. The bugles play a lively tune that gives the troops new energy in spite of the heat.

That morning, Dolley orders dinner to be ready at 3 o'clock, as usual. She is sure the president and his guests will be celebrating an American victory today. She wants the meal to be special. Elegant. Paul Jennings, the president's 15-year-old personal servant, an enslaved young boy, sets the table himself. He lugs ale, cider, and wine from the cellar and places them into coolers. Then he gathers the finest silver, plates, and glasses. In the kitchen, the fireplaces are lit. Spits loaded with meats turn around and around. Pots and pans sit on the grate, ready to be filled.

Meanwhile, Private John Kennedy is about to drop. Still in his dancing shoes, he has been marching through the night. "I slept as I walked." Finally, the exhausted men are allowed to get some shut-eye. But all too soon they are up and headed toward the town of Bladensburg, Maryland—a mere five miles from Washington.

By 10 a.m. the British have made it to Bladensburg, too. The troops are beginning to stagger. Many have fallen behind. General Ross realizes they must rest and gives the order to halt. Lieutenant George Gleig later recalls, "We threw ourselves upon the grass and in five minutes the mass of the army was asleep. My eyes were closed before my head hit the ground . . ."

Eager for battle, Ross wakes them up just an hour later. Time to move ahead.

Wednesday, August 24, 1814
Noon

The two armies advance, closer and closer, closing the gap. Suddenly, they can see each other across the Potomac River. Only a narrow bridge separates them. On one side, row after row of well-trained British troops in their red uniforms. Among them is Lieutenant George Gleig. On the other side, among the trees, the Americans stand ready, some in coats and jackets and some in blue uniforms. Among them is Private John Pendleton Kennedy. This mismatched group is all that stands between the enemy and America's capital, but they are confident they will win.

Equally confident are the British.

Wednesday, August 24, 1814
Afternoon

The Americans are not well trained, but they are enthusiastic. And very patriotic. They are good shots, too. Hunting deer, squirrels, pigeons, and bullfrogs makes them sharpshooters. Shouting and hollering, they bravely face the enemy across the wooden bridge.

Ready, aim, FIRE!

On the other side of the river, the command rings out: *Forward, forward!* Admiral Cockburn, mounted on his white horse, is in plain sight. An officer warns him to take cover. His answer: "Nonsense!" Suddenly, a shot hits the side of his saddle, just missing his leg. Lieutenant Gleig is not as lucky. A bullet pierces him in the arm, but he keeps moving forward.

Then comes the big surprise.

The sounds of battle shatter the air. They can be heard inside the White House. As the thunder of gunfire rages on, Dolley writes, "Will you believe it, my sister? . . . Here I am still, within sound of the cannon! Mr. Madison comes not. May God protect us!" Suddenly, James Smith, a formerly enslaved African, gallops up to the White House. Covered in dust and waving his hat, he cries, "Clear out, clear out!" The American general has ordered his troops to retreat!

On the battlefield, waves of redcoats keep pouring across the bridge, stepping over the bodies of their dead countrymen. Private Kennedy falls back with his fellow American soldiers. His fancy shoes are still on his feet. But there will be no invitation to a party at the White House today.

By 4:00, the battle is over.
The Americans are defeated.

Word of the defeat spreads like a swarm of bees. A family
friend bursts into the White House and begs Dolley to flee.
The rumor is that Admiral Cockburn will burn the house
over her head if he finds her there.

Paul Jennings looks on as confusion hits the White House.
People running in and out. Carriages racing by on the streets.
In the chaos, Dolley orders her carriage to be made ready.
But there is one last thing she insists on doing.

The clock is ticking.

Admiral Cockburn and his troops regroup to rest and care for their wounded. They will wait for dusk to make their next move.

Will that give Dolley enough time to escape?

"Save the painting!" orders Dolley. The large portrait of George Washington must not fall into British hands. White House servants struggle to unscrew the heavy painting from the wall, but it is taking too long. Dolley shouts for an ax to break the frame. *Chop! Whack!* It works. The painting is whisked away to safety, as Dolley races to her carriage.

The British wait like nighttime predators. When the coolness of evening sets in, they will enter Washington. After all, what's the rush? No one will block their way.

Wednesday, August 24, 1814
Evening

Less than an hour later, the president arrives at the White House. Outside, people are running in every direction. Weary American troops flee in confusion—running, hobbling, creeping, panic-stricken. Finding his dear Dolley gone, James dashes off a message and sends it to his wife. He will meet her at a friend's house in Virginia. The White House servants drive off in coaches. They stop only to leave Polly the macaw with a neighbor. The president rides off. Paul Jennings soon follows.

Paul turns to give a last look. He is shocked. People are running into the White House to steal whatever they can. Will anything be left when he returns?

The British soldiers have rested long enough. As darkness falls, Admiral Cockburn and General Ross lead about 100 troops into Washington. They are ready to take the city.

Wednesday, August 24, 1814
Night

Michael Shiner, the 9-year-old boy enslaved by a prominent Washington family, ventures outside. He can't believe his eyes. The British army is marching over the hill. Their feet sound like drumbeats. Their red coats and the red stocks of their guns look like flames of fire. Michael turns and runs.

Seeing no signs of the enemy, Cockburn and Ross order the troops to halt in front of the Capitol Building. They are ready to negotiate the terms of the surrender. The drummer gives the signal—a long, loud drumroll. Silence. No one appears. Of course not—the government has fled. Another drumroll sounds. This time there is a response. Shots ring out from a house across the way. A British officer's horse is shot dead under him. One soldier is killed, and another is wounded. Negotiations? No way! Now the British are out for revenge.

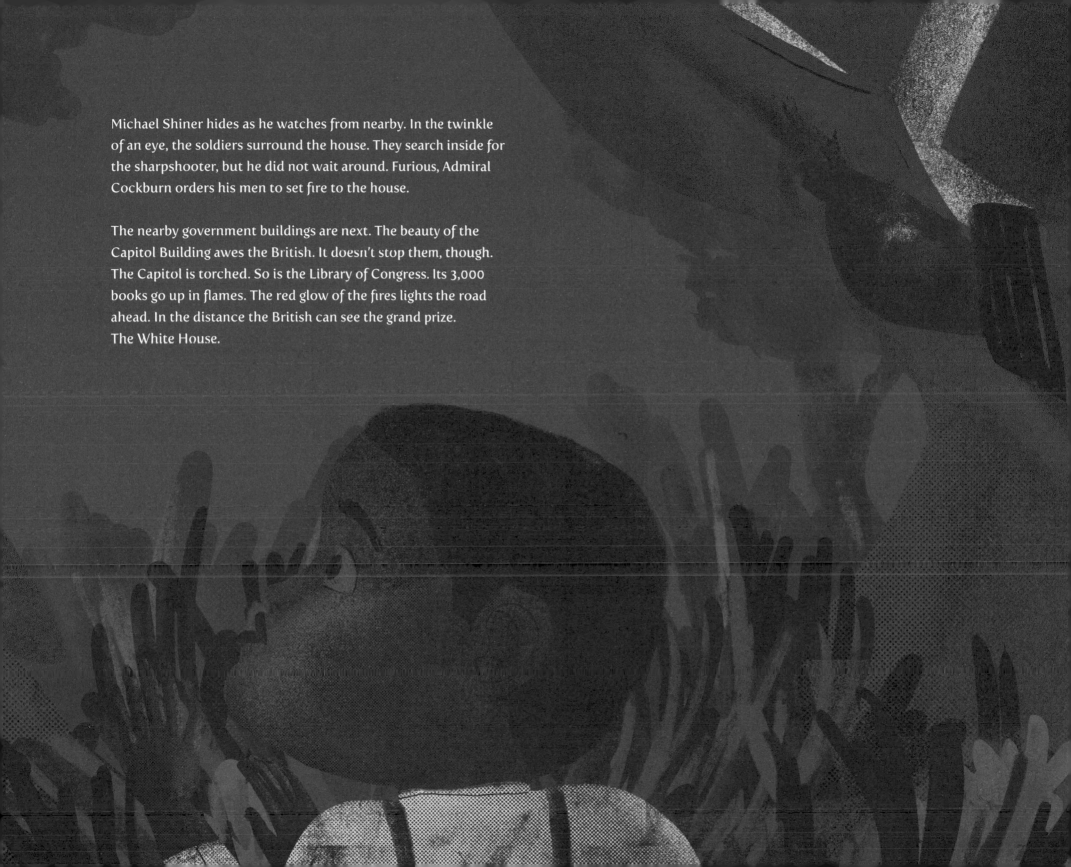

Michael Shiner hides as he watches from nearby. In the twinkle of an eye, the soldiers surround the house. They search inside for the sharpshooter, but he did not wait around. Furious, Admiral Cockburn orders his men to set fire to the house.

The nearby government buildings are next. The beauty of the Capitol Building awes the British. It doesn't stop them, though. The Capitol is torched. So is the Library of Congress. Its 3,000 books go up in flames. The red glow of the fires lights the road ahead. In the distance the British can see the grand prize. The White House.

It is an hour before midnight. Admiral Cockburn delays no longer. With their men, he and General Ross head down Pennsylvania Avenue to the home of Dolley and the president. As they break into the deserted mansion, they are struck by a delicious smell. Dolley's victory dinner is there, cooked and ready to eat. What luck! What a feast! The weary, uninvited guests dig in.

Afterward, a few officers snoop around upstairs. In James Madison's dressing room they spot some snowy clean shirts. More good luck! They change into them, leaving behind their own dirty, sweaty tops. Meanwhile, downstairs Ross and Cockburn order the soldiers to stack the furniture on the dining room table. They pull down the remaining drapes and pile them on top. What is to become of the White House?

The White House is set ablaze.

The British continue their destruction of America's capital. The Treasury Building is soon wrapped in flames. The other public buildings can wait until the morning to be torched. Admiral Cockburn is satisfied with the night's work. He feels generous, so he does not touch private homes. And he orders, *No looting!* Time to return to his headquarters for a few hours of sleep.

The night sky is as bright as day. The winds of a coming storm whip in. They fan the flames, making them burn even stronger and brighter.

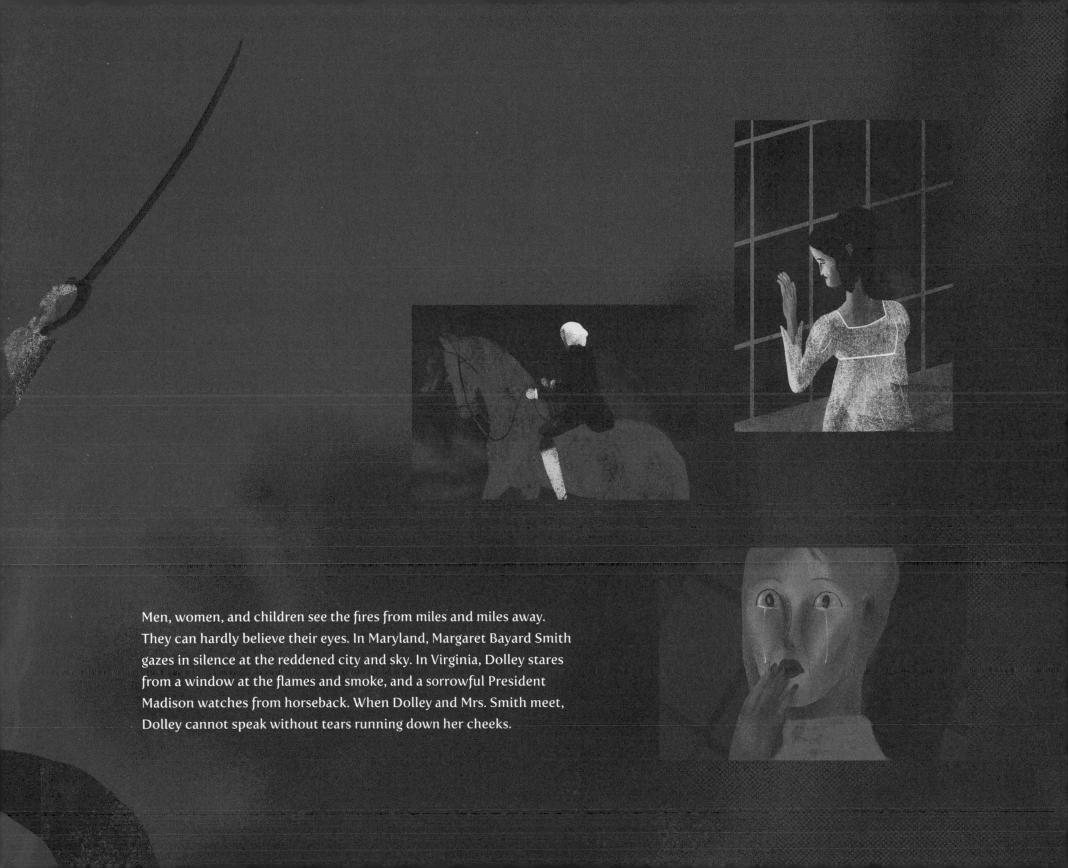

Men, women, and children see the fires from miles and miles away. They can hardly believe their eyes. In Maryland, Margaret Bayard Smith gazes in silence at the reddened city and sky. In Virginia, Dolley stares from a window at the flames and smoke, and a sorrowful President Madison watches from horseback. When Dolley and Mrs. Smith meet, Dolley cannot speak without tears running down her cheeks.

Thursday, August 25, 1814
Morning

Admiral Cockburn is up at the crack of dawn. He rides once again into the city. He wants to see and be seen. Government buildings are smoldering. Columns of smoke rise from the ruins. More buildings are set ablaze.

Excellent! he thinks.

The few residents who have stayed in Washington are awake.
They stare in horror at their beloved city.

Thursday, August 25, 1814
Afternoon

Suddenly, the afternoon sky grows as dark as midnight. The winds are
wilder than the night before. They sweep in a violent thunderstorm.
And with it comes something even more destructive. A tornado.

Roofs of houses are torn off. They are whisked into the air like sheets of paper. Trees, stones, and bricks fly like feathers. Lieutenant Gleig sees two cannons lifted off the ground and flung several yards away. Buildings crash to the ground. The rain pounds like a mighty waterfall. The thunder is deafening. The storm continues for two hours.

When the rain hits the hot walls of the burning government buildings, they crack. Some collapse. But luckily, the downpour puts out the flames, and the fires do not spread.

The storm saves Washington from total destruction.

Wednesday, August 24, 1814
Night

It's 8 o'clock, and all the residents hurry indoors. There will be trouble if they don't obey Admiral Cockburn's order—a curfew.

A rumor reaches Cockburn and Ross. Fresh American troops are gathering outside the city. Are they planning another attack? British soldiers are exhausted and in no shape to continue fighting. The two leaders agree: Why stay? They have achieved their goal. It would be smart to leave now. But it must be done in absolute secrecy. They pass the word along: Be ready to march after dark. Do not say a word. Do not make a sound. The British troops light their campfires as usual. Then they slip out in total silence. Even the ever-watchful Michael Shiner does not hear or see a thing.

Saturday, August 27, 1814

President Madison and Dolley return to the White House. What's the damage? Their home is just a shell surrounded by cracked and blackened walls. James and Dolley know they will never be able to live there. They will move to another residence. But what about a home for future presidents? What should be done?

There are many opinions. Move the capital to New York! Move it to Philadelphia! Stay and rebuild! James and Dolley insist the White House be rebuilt in the same place where it now stands. Congress finally agrees, and work begins.

Three years later, the White House is ready for a new president. And it still stands today as a symbol of our country. But those who look carefully can see signs of its history. Burn marks on some of the old stones tell the story. They remind us of what happened one night in August 1814.

In 1795, two stars and two stripes were added to the U.S. flag when the states of Kentucky and Vermont were added to our country. That made a total of 15 stars and 15 stripes. This was the U.S. flag until 1818, when Congress determined that the flag would have only 13 stripes for the original 13 colonies and one star for each state. This flag—with 15 stars and stripes—was the one flying over Fort McHenry during the War of 1812 and is the flag that inspired the writing of "The Star-Spangled Banner," our national anthem, by Francis Scott Key.

What Happened to Them?

Dolley Madison

Dolley became a celebrity! An ice cream was named after her. Newspapers reported on her doings. She was even honored with her own seat in the House of Representatives. Unheard of for a woman. When Dolley died at age 81, she had the largest funeral Washington had ever seen.

Today she'd have her own talk show.

James Madison

People blamed the president for the burning of Washington. They said he was a coward for fleeing the city. But when the United States won the war, joyful Americans forgave and forgot. At the end of his term, Madison moved back to his country home in Virginia along with his dear Dolley.

Paul Jennings called Madison "one of the best men who ever lived."

Admiral George Cockburn

He was a villain to Americans, but a hero back home. The man who burned Washington was elected to England's Parliament (legislative body). Later he became the head of the entire British Royal Navy.

Cockburn's destruction of the city of Washington horrified Americans in 1814 as much as the catastrophic attack of September 11, 2001, horrified us.

General Robert Ross

The general died in battle just a few weeks after he and his army torched Washington. His body was preserved in rum and shipped to the British colony of Nova Scotia. He was buried there.

His descendants were granted the honor to call themselves "Ross of Bladensburg."

Paul Jennings

Jennings, an enslaved man, had to go back to Virginia with the Madisons. After James died, Jennings expected Dolley to free him. But she needed money and sold Jennings instead. Jennings managed to save enough and bought his freedom by the time he was 48 years old. Devoted to the president, Jennings later published a memoir, *A Colored Man's Reminiscences of James Madison*. Jennings died a property owner in Washington. D. C.

He was the first writer of a behind-the-scenes look at the White House.

Lieutenant George Gleig

Thanks to Gleig, we have a blow-by-blow account of the War of 1812 from the British point of view. He wrote another fifty-seven books, including some novels, before he died at the age of 92.

He was an eyewitness to history.

Private John Pendleton Kennedy

After leaving the army, Kennedy became a lawyer. However, he decided he liked writing and politics better. He was successful at both. His books were popular during his time, and he served in the U.S. House of Representatives and as Secretary of the Navy. Despite being born in the South, Kennedy supported President Lincoln and the Union during the Civil War.

First known for his dancing shoes, he was later known for his pen.

Michael Shiner

Years after the British invaded Washington, Michael Shiner wrote about it in a diary. Nobody during his lifetime knew about his book. Where did he learn to read and write? In his church Sunday school, the only schools enslaved Africans were allowed to attend. Shiner was finally able to buy his freedom when he was an adult. He became a well-known leader in his community.

When President Lincoln signed the Emancipation Proclamation, Shiner declared, "The only master I have now is the Constitution."

Margaret Bayard Smith

Today, we would call Mrs. Smith a Washington "insider." She went everywhere and knew everybody. And she was always writing about her observations and experiences in her letters and notebooks. Dolley Madison, as well as Thomas Jefferson, remained her lifelong friends. In the 1820s, Smith began publishing her novels and poetry. But long after she died, her grandson came upon her letters. He found them among 3,500 pieces of her writing! He had them published in a book called *The First Forty Years of Washington Society*.

She would have made a great newspaper reporter.

The City Before It Was Torched

It's thanks to President George Washington that the city of Washington is located where it is. He chose its site on the Potomac River.

It was the vision of Frenchman Pierre Charles L'Enfant that gave the United States a capital of grand buildings and wide streets. At the center would be the Capitol Building on Pennsylvania Avenue framed by poplar trees.

The illustration at right shows L'Enfant's vision of what the Capitol would look like when it was finished. But by 1811, money for the building was being used for the war with Great Britain. So the two wings of the building were connected by a temporary wooden walkway. This is the structure that the British army set fire to on the night of August 24, 1814.

The White House stood at the other end of Pennsylvania Avenue.

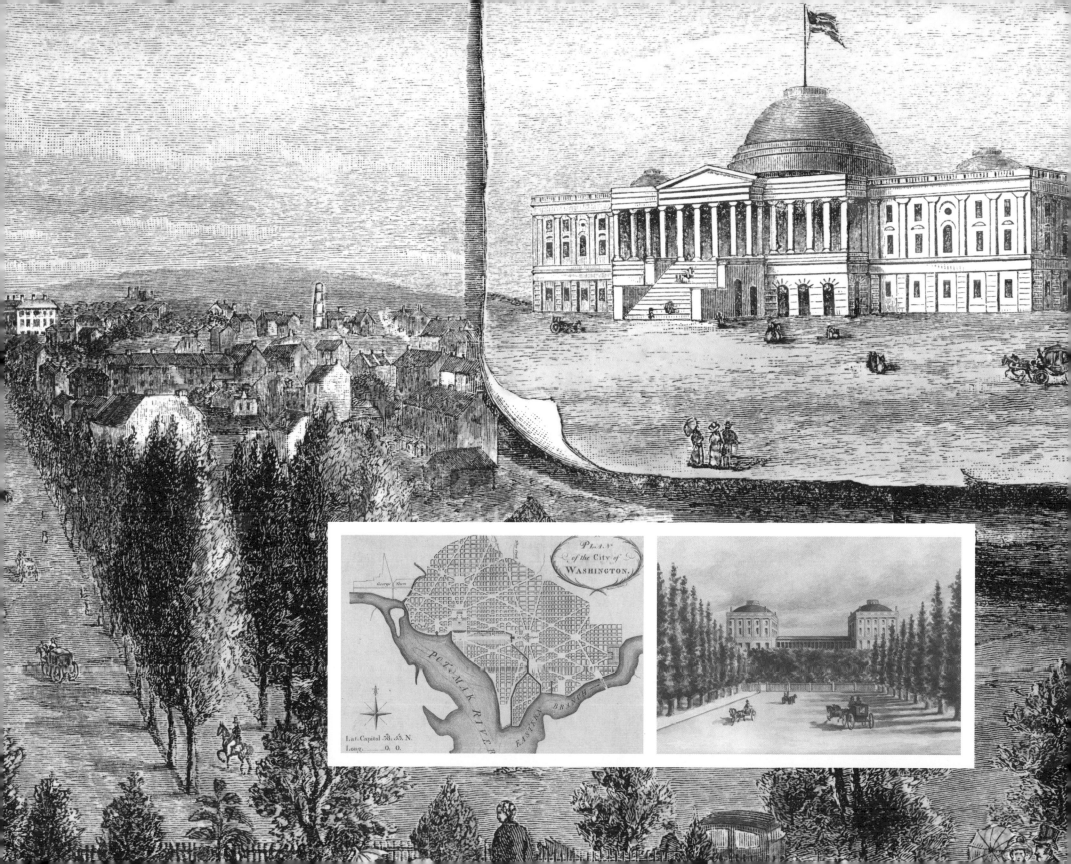

PLAN of the City of WASHINGTON.

POTOMAK RIVER

EASTERN BRANCH

George Town

Lat. Capitol 58. 55. N.
Long.   0. 0.

Pennsylvania Avenue is shown in an engraving of the time. The Capitol Building would
be at one end and the president's house at the other, a mile and a half away.

The U.S. Treasury Building was another of the many government buildings that the British torched. It was also located on Pennsylvania Avenue, very close to the White House.

They Had a Ball!

Dolley Madison loved a good party. She attended a very special one when James Madison was elected as the fourth president of the United States. On the night of Madison's inauguration, the nation held its first Inaugural Ball to honor the new president. That started a tradition that continues to this day (except in 2021 due to the COVID-19 pandemic).

The ball was organized in just five days by twelve men who were good friends of James and Dolley. It was held at the newly opened Long's Hotel on Capitol Hill on March 4, 1809. Tickets cost $4. More than four hundred people attended the event, which the *National Intelligencer* newspaper described as "the most brilliant and crowded ever known in Washington."

One of the guests was Margaret Bayard Smith, who later wrote an enthusiastic account of the scene. Dolley was clearly the center of attention.

"It was scarcely possible to elbow your way from one side to another, and poor Mrs. Madison was almost pressed to death, for every one crowded round her, those behind pressing on those before, and peeping over their shoulders to have a peep of her, and those who were so fortunate as to get near enough to speak to her were happy indeed."

Mrs. Smith goes on to describe what Mrs. Madison wore.

"She looked a queen. She had on a pale buff colored velvet, made plain, with a very long train, but not the least trimming, and beautiful pearl necklace, earrings and bracelets. Her head dress was a turban of the same coloured velvet and white satin (from Paris) with two superb plumes, the bird of paradise feathers."

When the dancing began, the crowded ballroom became unbearably hot. People began to feel faint, but for some reason the windows would not open. The solution? The glass window panes had to be broken!

At the stroke of midnight, the music and dancing stopped. Guests began to leave in their coaches. The first Inaugural Ball had ended.

Right: In 1900, American painter and illustrator Jennie Augusta Brownscombe (1850–1936) captured the event in a painting she titled *Dolly Madison's Ball*. It is currently owned by the Huntsville Museum of Art (in Alabama), which has graciously given the Dolley Madison Digital Edition (DMDE) permission to include it here.

Inset: A photo of the gown Dolley Madison wore to the first Inaugural Ball in 1809.

It's War!

President James Madison signed a Declaration of War against Great Britain on June 18, 1812. A Maryland newspaper carried the dreadful news a week later.

But why did America, a brand-new country, risk going to war with powerful Great Britain? One reason was that Great Britain was interfering with American shipping across the Atlantic. Another reason was that British naval officers were boarding American ships looking for British sailors who might have been deserters. Suspected sailors were seized and forced to join the British Navy. But many American sailors were seized as well. Finally, Great Britain was supplying weapons to some of the Native Americans who were trying to protect their lands.

Peace!

A peace treaty was signed by American and British representatives in Europe on December 24, 1814. But no one in America knew it—not the president, not the generals, not the people. Today, of course, it would be breaking news on the Internet, social media, and TV. In 1814, however, a special messenger had to bring the peace treaty by ship across the Atlantic. It took a month to make the trip.

So on January 8, 1815, both armies were still fighting and dying—needlessly. In the last big battle of the war, American troops were victorious. More than 2,000 redcoats died or were wounded. About 80 Americans suffered the same fate. It was a total waste of lives; the war had already ended. President James Madison signed the peace treaty on February 17, 1815.

Top: Dolley Madison Directing the Rescue of George Washington's Portrait, August 24, 1814. William Woodward, artist. 2009. Courtesy of The Montpelier Foundation.
Left: Portrait of George Washington by Gilbert Stuart (1796). Oil on canvas, 95 x 60 inches.

History or Myth?

Over time, stories told orally, from one person to the next, can change. Interesting details can be added or removed. Facts can be exaggerated. The same sometimes happens when people tell about events from history. An actual event can turn into something bigger and more exciting than what really happened. It can become a myth.

The story of Dolley Madison saving the famous painting of George Washington has been told for over 200 years. As the story is commonly told, Dolley has the painting hurriedly removed and then flees the White House clutching it in her arms. But is it true?

On August 24, 1814, Dolley wrote a letter to her sister about saving the George Washington painting. In this letter she wrote:

"Our kind friend, Mr. Carroll, has come to hasten my departure, and is in a very bad humor with me because I insist on waiting until the large picture of General Washington is secured, and it requires to be unscrewed from the wall. This process was found too tedious for these perilous moments; I have ordered the frame to be broken, and the canvass taken out; it is done—and the precious portrait placed in the hands of two gentlemen of New York, for safe keeping."

Clearly, Dolley's first account of the event is different from the story often told. She says nothing about clutching the painting as she runs out of the White House for her safety. Instead, she hands the painting to two men from New York. But by 1831, the story she told in her letter had already changed. Here's what someone wrote about that important moment in history as he "heard" it:

"We drove to the palace (White House), entered . . . a drawing-room, in which is a fine full-length picture of General Washington. When the British came here in the last war, the President was obliged to fly. His wife, Mrs. Madison, cut the picture from the frame and took it with her—the only article she took!"

And so the myth of Dolley racing away with the painting became commonly told. But Paul Jennings, who was an enslaved man in the household of James and Dolley Madison, and was present on that day, wrote his memories of the event in 1865 in his autobiography. He wrote:

"It has often been stated in print, that when Mrs. Madison escaped from the White House, she cut out from the frame the large portrait of Washington . . . and carried it off. This is totally false. She had no time for doing it. It would have required a ladder to get it down . . . . John Susé [Jean-Pierre Sioussat, the doorkeeper] . . . and Magraw, the President's gardener, took it down and sent it off on a wagon, with some large silver urns and such other valuables as could be hastily got hold of."

So what really happened? All we know for sure is that the painting was saved under the direction of Dolley Madison and remains in the White House today for visitors to see. Many think the story changed because the story of a brave Dolley Madison fleeing the White House with the iconic painting of our first president in her arms is too exciting not to tell. And as such, the myth continues today.

Signs of the Past

Even though the events described in this book took place long ago, you can see evidence that they really happened. How? Scorch marks left by the fire are still visible today on the White House. Fire-blackened stones above two of the entrances have been left unpainted. You might never notice them unless someone points them out to you. But they give us a glimpse into what happened one night in August 1814 and remind us of a dark time in our country's history.

As one visitor recounted, "I was fascinated when one of the guards pointed out to us that the lintel over the door to the basement showed burn marks and bullet holes that were still there from the War of 1812, when the White House burned down. That is certainly a piece of history that not many people see."
(Claire Jones, 2011)

Bibliography

Allgor, Catherine. *A Perfect Union: Dolley Madison and the Creation of the American Nation.* New York: Henry Holt, 2006.

"Dolley Madison's Letters to Her Sister, August 23 and 24, 1814." In *Dolly Madison* by Maud Wilder Goodwin. New York: C. Scribner's Sons, 1896, pp. 173–175.

"Dolley Madison to Mary Latrobe, December 3, 1814." The White House Historical Association: "Saving History: Dolley Madison, the White House and the War of 1812." https://www.nps.gov/common/uploads/teachers/lessonplans/STSP%20Primary%20Document.pdf.

Gleig, George R. *The Campaigns of the British Army at Washington and New Orleans, in the Years 1814–1815.* London: John Murray, 1821.

———. *A Subaltern in America; Comprising His Narrative of the Campaigns of the British Army, at Baltimore, Washington, &c. &c. During the Late War.* Philadelphia & Boston, 1833.

Hickey, Donald R., ed. *The War of 1812: Writings from America's Second War of Independence.* New York: Library of America, 2013.

Jennings, Paul. *A Colored Man's Reminiscences of James Madison.* Brooklyn: George C. Beadle, 1865.

Niles' Weekly Register. August 21, 1813.

Pack, James. *The Man Who Burned the White House: Admiral Sir George Cockburn, 1772–1853.* Emsworth, UK: Kenneth Mason, 1987.

Scott, James. *Recollections of a Naval Life.* London: Richard Bentley, 1834.

Shiner, Michael. "The Diary of Michael Shiner Relating to the History of the Washington Navy Yard 1813–1869." Transcribed With Introduction and Notes by John G. Sharp. http://www.ibiblio.org/hyperwar/NHC/shiner/shiner_diary.htm.

Smith, Margaret Bayard. *The First Forty Years of Washington Society: Portrayed by the Family Letters of Mrs. Samuel Harrison Smith (Margaret Bayard) from the Collection of Her Grandson, J. Henley Smith.* Edited by Gaillard Hunt. New York: C. Scribner's Sons, 1906.

Snow, Peter. *When Britain Burned the White House: The 1814 Invasion of Washington.* New York: St. Martin's Press, 2014.

Sutcliffe, Jane. *The White House Is Burning: August 24, 1814.* Watertown, MA: Charlesbridge, 2014.

Tuckerman, Henry T. *The Life of John Pendleton Kennedy.* New York: G. P. Putnam & Sons, 1871.

Articles

"America Under Fire: Aftermath." The White House Historical Association.
https://www.whitehousehistory.org/america-under-fire-aftermath.

"Dolley Payne Madison: First Lady." http://www.dolleymadison.org.

Fleming, Thomas. "When Dolley Madison Took Command of the White House."
Smithsonian Magazine, March 2010. http://www.smithsonianmag.com/
history/how-dolley-madison-saved-the-day-7465218/.

"Madison Reconstruction: 1814–1817." The White House Museum.
http://www.whitehousemuseum.org/special/renovation-1814.htm.

"The Burning of Washington." The White House Historical Association.
https://www.whitehousehistory.org/the-burning-of-washington.

"This Day in Weather History: August 25th."
https://www.weather.gov/abr/This_Day_in_Weather_History_Aug_25.

Zielinski, Sarah. "The Tornado That Saved Washington." *Smithsonian
Magazine,* August 25, 2010. http://www.smithsonianmag.com/science-
nature/the-tornado-that-savedwashington-33901211/?no-ist.

Alice Boynton

loves history. For her, reading about people and events from the past is not just interesting, it's exciting—especially when she can find out what happened from the words of the people who were on the scene at the time. Alice hopes to bring to her readers the excitement of being an eyewitness to history.

Wiley Blevins

is a writer living in New York City. He has written many nonfiction books for children as well as books for teachers on how to teach nonfiction text structures and features. Wiley's other books include *Sunday with Savta* and *Trevor Lee and the Big Uh-Oh!*

Massimiliano di Lauro

is an award-winning Italian illustrator based in Puglia, Italy. He has published children's books and worked in animation.